Sally Weans From Night Nursing

By
Lesli Mitchell, LCSW

ISBN-13: 978-1483933832 (paperback)
ISBN-10: 1483933830 (paperback)
LCNN # 2013908857

DEDICATION

This book is dedicated to my daughter Ava and her father Earnest Mitchell. All three of us worked very hard to accomplish night weaning and I am proud of us! This is also in dedication to my beautiful parents Susan Anne Kehrli Rogers and my dear Father William Devon Rogers, may he rest in peace. This is also in dedication to Ernie's mom, Geneva Lewis, a loving grandmother and mother-in-law. Also thanks to my brothers and sisters, Jennifer Cherry, William Symons-Rogers, and Glenys Rogers, for their feedback and support. And lastly, this is in dedication to all the mothers adjusting to being moms and all the love they give in the process.

INTRODUCTION

I did not originally plan on night nursing my child for 23 months. We were not going to have another child and I wasn't going back to work right away, so there was no outside pressure to stop nursing. I really wasn't sure how to stop night nursing, so I just kept on doing what seemed to be the easiest thing for a somewhat restful night. When she was a newborn, I would get up about every hour, sit on the edge of my bed and nurse her next to her bassinet. When she was old enough, she began sleeping in a little sturdy bed in my bed and continued nursing on demand. The nursing on demand at night continued until she was almost two years old.

I began to start feeling really sleep deprived when she became more active in the day. The cumulative impact of being sleep deprived every night since her birth began to take its toll. She was a very active toddler, and at some point, I realized it was time for me to stop the nightly "drink-drink" (as she called it). It became critical for us to transition from night nursing so that I could function in the day. I was exhausted and at times so was she. Part of it was my activity level, I didn't like staying home all day and playing, I was used to getting out and being active. To my detriment, I also didn't take naps in the daytime with her so I was super exhausted. I wanted to nap but she only would take a nap while latched on to me, and I needed a break from it. So, I opted to drive around in my car to put her to sleep, just to have some personal time. I didn't want to nurse her to sleep in the day because I would also have to lay down or she would wake up. I probably technically needed to take a nap, but I really just wanted some personal space. She took 1 ½ hour naps pretty much only while I was driving her around in the car. Where was the break? I found myself feeling less energy to play with her, engage with her and be present with her. I didn't want to be exhausted and irritated all day.

I began to consider the concept of changing our system. I began to sort out the hard facts of the situation. First and foremost, she did not need my milk for her survival any longer because she was eating solid food. The nurturing and bonding during night nursing was lovely, but it was starting to negatively impact our day bonding and connectedness. I figured she could still get my attention, love and bonding if she wakes up at night, but we would have to find another way besides nursing. My husband reminded me that he would help in the transition by giving his love and affection to help her cope with the change. I figured she was still able to nurse in the day, so the nursing pleasure wasn't all taken away in one giant swipe. With all the sleep deprivation, it was hard to think through all of this clearly, but I finally got there in my own way because I had to. This process required me to look at all the pros and cons, assess my own personal emotional state and readiness, my family situation/support and the actual needs of my child. It helped that I had a few close friends that were also night nursing and considering when to wean, so they were going through a similar experience.

Although it was helpful to lay out all of the facts of our situation, I nevertheless felt totally emotionally overwhelmed at the thought of night weaning. I had gotten into a familiar way of coping and it was scary to think of changing anything that seemed to be working. How else would I get her back to sleep without nursing? I was afraid that I would be even more exhausted if I stopped nursing at night. There is always the fear that your change might not work and potentially make everything worse. I felt like I was already hanging on by a thin thread, why would I disrupt my system? And then there was the feeling of guilt for my single child, why couldn't I just do this indefinitely for her and let it phase out naturally? I didn't want her to experience any losses at such a young age. Would she be emotionally impacted by this night weaning event?

So, as many parents do, I had to sit with all of my feelings and make the best decision. I waffled and wavered for a few months, before I was very clear that it was time. Once I decided that it was okay to help my daughter transition through her feelings, I was ready. I figured this was one of our big emotional transitions together and I began to feel honored that I was going to be the one to gently guide us through it. Part of it was that I had not assumed a leadership role yet. My daughter and I were just in this co-sleeping, night nursing relationship together, no one was managing it or running it per se. My sister once told me that children are flexible and that concept helped me during this time. With such a long history of routine and identity, adults are often the ones that are less flexible. Babies are just starting out and though they may resist, in the end they are way more flexible and open to change than we are. With children, it is not set in stone, you just have to support and help them move to the next stage and believe in your leadership role to guide change. This is actually only one of the many transitions you will be guiding your child through. As an adult, I saw the bigger picture and I needed to guide us through to the next phase in our mother/daughter relationship. It is such a personal decision, no one can tell you when you should be ready or when you have to wean. However, what I found is that I was more apt to be consistent and actually follow through when I felt truly grounded in my decision.

In my search to find a gentle approach to weaning, I found a book called "The No-Cry Sleep Solution" by Elizabeth Pantley. The author suggested that the parent write a child friendly book about weaning from night nursing. So, as an artist and a person who enjoys writing, this was right up my alley. That night, I sat down with a serious purpose at the kitchen table and wrote and sketched out the first draft. My daughter was receptive to the story, and so I decided to illustrate a more colorful version with references to some of her toys and specific bedtime routines. Ironically, I illustrated and wrote this book while she was napping in the car, overlooking several fabulous views in Laguna beach.

It became a daily ritual to read Ava the Sally book. In fact, she began to ask for it regularly. It was my plan to get the concept into her thought process so that the idea was not so abrupt and foreign. Reading the Sally book to Ava was a way that my husband and I could introduce the idea of night weaning in a gentle and fun way. I found that reading the book a few times per day to Ava and then right before bed was helpful in our process of weaning. Ava could understand the ideas in the book, so that when I told her we would nurse in the morning, she had a context with which to understand the new changes. Ava could identify with the character Sally and was able to develop some understanding as to why weaning needed to happen. I liked that Ava had a chance to understand what was happening instead of just having it happen to her. Sally is a third party character to rely upon during those tough midnight weaning moments. Sally is more removed from the emotionally charged relationship between mommy and child. Sally is just sharing her story with your child. Sally was an additional voice, a little cartoon friend in the night, to reinforce and validate the journey of night weaning.

Deciding when to night wean your child is such a personal decision. I am writing this book because I found it helpful to have a gentle tool to help my child understand what was happening in her world. She was old enough to actually comprehend the concept of weaning on some level and why it needed to happen. Sally's story helped validate and mirror Ava's feelings, which in and of itself can be a soothing experience. Although difficult and exhausting at times, nursing my child has been a wonderful, beautiful bonding experience for us both.

HOW WE DID IT:
STEP BY STEP

I must say that my husband was a big help. It was very hard for me to hear her crying and screaming, begging to nurse. My husband assured me that his presence was loving and soothing for her. He reminded me that even though she wasn't getting what she wanted from mommy—she still had Daddy. I know that not everyone has a partner that is available to help or willing to help, so, this is not a one size fits all model. There can be other things are soothing, it doesn't have to be daddy/mommy. Other things can be a back rub, a special blanket/toy to hug that you buy for the event. I like the idea of planning with your child what is going to happen and how you will both cope with it. So, use pieces of this model that work for your family and modify aspects of it to fit your situation.

I did a few things in preparation for the event.

First off, I made sure I was the adult in the situation and I was going to hold to my thought that it IS the time to wean and that it is important for my bonding with her in the day time.

A few months prior to weaning, I stopped nursing her to sleep at night and my husband took over. He began rocking her before bed, so that she would get used to falling asleep another way and with another person. She really protested, but she slowly began adjusting to the change. She needed another way to fall asleep aside from nursing, so we had to provide another way. My husband would read the Sally book before bed and I would read it in the day. Another way could be another close relative rocking her to sleep or giving her a new big boy or big girl toy to sleep with, back rubbing, mommy sings a song, etc.

Instead of nursing in the bedroom, I nursed in a special nursing chair that was outside of the room we slept in. It seemed important to try to break the association between our bedroom and nursing.

When we felt like it was about the right time to begin the weaning process, it helped to actually schedule a time to make it happen. We looked at our schedules and organized the amount of time and dates that would really work for both of us. It helped to make a date, because we also needed to psychologically prepare for this huge event that was going to change our families routine. Also, when you schedule time, you tend to be more committed to the task. My husband used his vacation and took off one week, so that there was not concern about being able to function the next day if she was up all night screaming. So, when she would wake up, I would talk to her about Sally, about how just like Sally we need to wait until morning to nurse. I would offer to rub her back like Sally in the book. If I was unable to comfort her and convince her to nurse in the morning, then my husband would come and comfort her and rock her. In those times, it was best that I left the room, because it was too upsetting for her to see me and not be able to nurse. My husband was able to take a week off from work to achieve our goal. I made sure I didn't have any important appointments for which I needed to be alert just in case I was going to be up all night. My husband and I felt comfortable that it would probably be completed within one week if we stayed consistent. Night weaning was completed in approximately four days. Using his vacation time was not the most ideal, but it was worth it to get through this important family event together.

After no more nursing at night was established, Ava chose to have me to rub her back gently whenever she woke up at night. Afterall, Sally got her back rubbed instead of nursing when she woke up. I rubbed Ava's back every night when she woke up more out of habit for approximately two weeks. Finally, she stopped requesting it and just slept through the night. Of coarse I was slightly concerned that the back rubbing would become a habit, but it just wasn't as awesome as nursing, so that dynamic ended much quicker. I think Ava quickly realized that there was no need to wake up for a lame little back rub from an exhausted, zoned-out zombie Mama.

After she weaned from night nursing, we had a no more night nursing party just to make it really official. No turning back! In celebration, we made a little strawberry shortcake with homemade whip cream, angel food cake and strawberries, to celebrate her graduation from night nursing. To this day, she reads herself to sleep in her own room, falls asleep by herself and sleeps through the night with no problems.

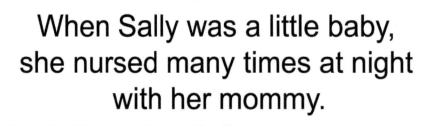

When Sally was a little baby,
she nursed many times at night
with her mommy.

Sally started to grow more and more.
Now Sally can eat with a fork and
drink from a cup. Sally isn't a baby anymore.

One day mommy said,
"Now that you are a big girl,
Mommy thinks you can sleep at night without nursing.
It might be hard, but let's try no more nursing at night."

Mommy said, "If we sleep at night,
we can do more fun things during the day.
I love you, Sally." Mommy gave Sally a big hug.

The next night, it was time for bed.
Sally took a bath, went potty and brushed her teeth.

Sally nursed with mommy right before bed.
Mommy reminded Sally,
"No more nursing once we go to sleep.
Mommy will nurse Sally in the morning.

Sally woke up at night and wanted to nurse.
Mommy said, "I am sorry, Sally, no more nursing at night.
It is time to sleep. I love you."

Sally felt sad. Sally cried because
she wanted to nurse, and Mommy said "no."

Sally felt angry, too. She said very loud,
"I want to nurse, Mommy!"

Mommy held Sally and said, " I know you are sad.
We will nurse in the morning when the sun comes up."
Sally said, "Okay Mommy, nurse in the morning
when the sun comes up."

Mommy rubs Sally's back
to help her go back to sleep.

Sally goes to sleep.

It's morning! Here comes the sun!
It's time to nurse in the special chair.

Mommy will take Sally to do fun things.
like blow bubbles.....

and fingerpaint.

Mommy and Sally don't feel tired anymore because they get a lot of sleep. Mommy and Sally dance together to music with pretty scarves!

Mommy gives Sally lots of hugs and kisses.
Mommy and Sally love each other very much.

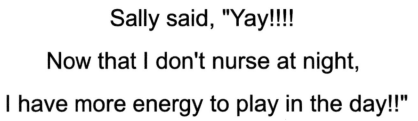

Sally said, "Yay!!!!

Now that I don't nurse at night,

I have more energy to play in the day!!"

ABOUT THE AUTHOR

Lesli Mitchell lives in Lake Forest, California with her husband Ernie and their daughter Ava. As of November 13, 2020, Ava is now 16 years old, a happy teen that loves to write, skateboard and play guitar. All that nursing was worth it!! Lesli is also the author of Sally Pone Fin a la Lactancia Nocturna (Spanish version) and Should I Make My Curly Hair Straight? Lesli is an Licensed Clinical Social Worker whom volunteers in the community and is the owner of Connect and Express, a creative tool for mental health professionals.

Made in United States
Troutdale, OR
10/09/2023

13557500R00019